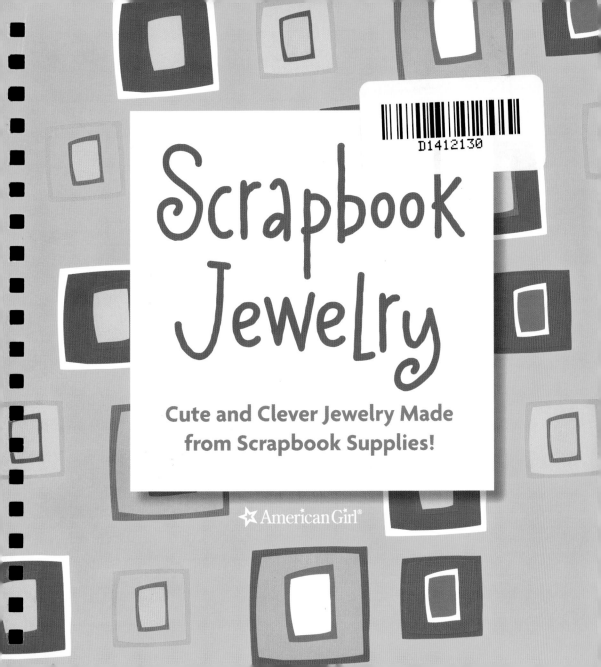

Scrapbook Jewelry

Cute and Clever Jewelry Made from Scrapbook Supplies!

★ American Girl®

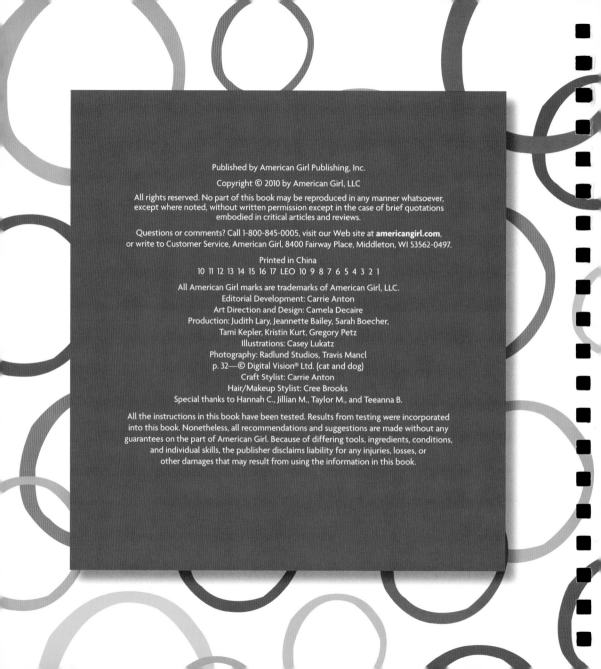

Published by American Girl Publishing, Inc.

Copyright © 2010 by American Girl, LLC

Questions or comments? Call 1-800-845-0005, visit our Web site at **americangirl.com**,
or write to Customer Service, American Girl, 8400 Fairway Place, Middleton, WI 53562-0497.

Printed in China
10 11 12 13 14 15 16 17 LEO 10 9 8 7 6 5 4 3 2 1

All American Girl marks are trademarks of American Girl, LLC.
Editorial Development: Carrie Anton
Art Direction and Design: Camela Decaire
Production: Judith Lary, Jeannette Bailey, Sarah Boecher,
Tami Kepler, Kristin Kurt, Gregory Petz
Illustrations: Casey Lukatz
Photography: Radlund Studios, Travis Mancl
p. 32—© Digital Vision® Ltd. (cat and dog)
Craft Stylist: Carrie Anton
Hair/Makeup Stylist: Cree Brooks
Special thanks to Hannah C., Jillian M., Taylor M., and Teeanna B.

Dear Reader,

If you like to scrapbook or just think scrapbook supplies are pretty, this book is for you! The projects in this book show you how to turn scrapbook supplies—such as decorative paper, stickers, chipboard pieces, and ribbon—into all kinds of accessories. Most of the projects can be completed with just a small amount of a few supplies—a great way to use up your scrapbooking leftovers! Or buy new supplies and gather friends together for a jewelry-making afternoon.

Your friends at American Girl

Scrapbook Supplies

Take a stroll down the scrapbook aisle, and you'll find super supplies to turn into great accessories to wear. Here are just a few used in this book.

Album tags are clear tiles with precut holes. They can be backed with paper so that the pattern shows through. They can be layered with stickers to act as charms. Or you can do both!

Chipboard is a special type of thick pressed paper similar to a thin cardboard. Chipboard pieces come in many basic shapes, such as rectangles, circles, and squares, as well as in precut shapes like butterflies, hearts, and animals. Chipboard pieces may be patterned, or you can decorate the plain ones with paper, stamps, or paint.

On a scrapbook page, an **adhesive frame** can border a picture or drawing, imitating a wall frame. Some scrapbook frames have a precut charm hole at the top, allowing you to also tie the frame to the page. This style of frame works great for jewelry as a picture pendant.

Show your personality, spell your name, or dress up something plain by simply sticking on **stickers.**

Ribbon and cord come in so many colors and widths! They work well for stringing pendants or for using on their own as embellishments.

And, of course, don't forget the **scrapbook paper!**

Jewelry Supplies

Scrapbook supplies are the decorative parts of the projects in this book, but jewelry supplies make the projects wearable.

A **jump ring** is a metal ring used to link jewelry pieces together. The ring is not a continuous circle—it can be opened and closed to hold jewelry pieces.

A **pad-post earring** has a flat surface so that you can attach something decorative.

Earring hooks are used to make dangly earrings. The wire hangs through a pierced ear, and the bottom has a small loop to hang things from.

A **jewelry hook** is a metal hook with a push arm you can open to slide on objects.

Elastic beading string is stretchy, so you can slip it on and off. To make a knot permanent, dab craft glue on the knot and let it dry.

A **head pin** is a piece of jewelry wire with one flat end so that you can thread on beads.

A **ball chain** is made up of small metal balls joined together by wire.

A **ball-chain clasp** joins two ends of a ball chain. The balls on each end slip and lock into each of the clasp openings.

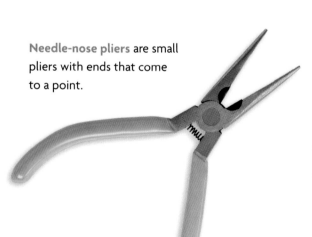

Needle-nose pliers are small pliers with ends that come to a point.

Note: The projects in this book should be able to be done without the use of pliers, but sometimes this tool comes in handy for closing jump rings and bending head pins. We've marked the projects where pliers may be needed with this symbol. Anytime you see this symbol—whether or not it indicates the use of pliers—you should always ask for an adult's help.

Bracelets

So Charming!

Create cool charms with patterned scrapbook paper and album tags.

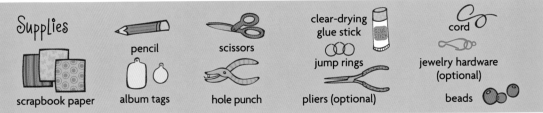

Supplies

pencil

scrapbook paper

album tags

scissors

hole punch

clear-drying glue stick

jump rings

pliers (optional)

cord

jewelry hardware (optional)

beads

To make charms:

1. On a piece of patterned scrapbook paper, trace the shape of one album tag, and mark the top circle. Cut out the shape. Use a small hole punch to punch the top circle opening in the paper.

2. Rub a thin layer of glue on the *back* of the album tag, and place it on the patterned side of the paper shape so that the edges line up. Let dry.

3. ☆ Open a jump ring and guide it through the top opening. Close by hand or ask an adult to close the ring with a pair of pliers.

To make a bracelet:

Cut a piece of cord long enough to fit around your wrist, plus extra length to either tie the cord closed or attach jewelry hardware to it. Tie a knot at one end, again leaving enough space for the closure of your choice. String on charms and coordinating beads until the cord is filled. Tie an end knot close to the final charm or bead.

rectangular
chipboard piece

embellishments
(optional)

hole punch
(optional)

ribbon

scissors

"Say It" Bracelet

When you wear your words, you say them with style!

Start with a rectangular chipboard piece that is no wider than your wrist. The chipboard can have a preprinted design, or you can embellish a plain piece of chipboard with scrapbook paper, stickers, or adhesive gems. If the chipboard is not prepunched, make a hole on each side of the rectangle with a hole punch (you may need help from an adult). String one piece of ribbon through each hole. Tie a knot (so that the knot sits on the top of the chipboard), or wrap the ribbon around and glue the end to the reverse side of the ribbon. Let dry. Trim the ribbon strands so that they are just long enough to tie in a bow around your wrist.

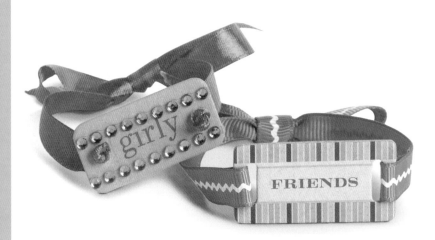

Roller Beads

Try this new *spin* on making a unique bracelet.

Supplies

ruler

pencil

elastic
beading string

scissors

scrapbook paper

glue stick

craft glue

To roll a bead:

Cut out a 1-by-3-inch rectangle from scrapbook paper.
Roll the rectangle tightly
around a pencil. Slide the
pencil out. Glue the end of
the paper closed, holding it
a few seconds until dry.

To make a bracelet:

1. Make about 18 beads.
Cut 4 feet of elastic beading string. Guide one bead
on the string and center it.

3. Insert left end of string into
left side of the same bead, and
pull through (see diagram). Pull
ends tight. Repeat steps 2 and
3 for each bead.

2. Stack a second bead on
the first. Thread right end
of string into right side of
bead, and pull through.

4. To finish, loop bracelet
around and pull end of string
through first bead once. Tie
tightly. Trim extra string. Dab
knot with craft glue. Let dry.

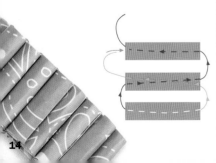

Supplies

wax paper

scrapbook paper

small foam
paintbrush

decoupage glue

plastic bangle
bracelet

Tear and stick your way to a paper-wrapped bracelet!

Since you'll be working with sticky stuff, start by covering your work surface with wax paper. Tear small strips of scrapbook paper no wider than your plastic bangle bracelet. With a small foam paintbrush, spread a thin coat of decoupage glue over your bracelet. Then spread a thin coat of decoupage glue on the back of a torn paper strip. Layer the paper on the bracelet and then apply another thin coat of decoupage glue. Repeat these steps until the entire bracelet is covered. Let dry.

Sipping-Straw Beads

Drinking straws and pretty paper are a great jewelry combo!

Supplies

pencil

scrapbook paper

glue stick

ball chain & clasp

pattern on page 50

scissors

drinking straws

beads

To Make the beads:

1. Using the pattern on page 50, trace and cut out one triangle from scrapbook paper for each bead. Cover the back of each triangle with glue.

2. Place the wide end of a triangle on the straw, with "glue side" to the straw. Tightly roll the paper. Repeat this step, filling the straw with as many triangles as fit.

3. Snip off the beads by cutting the straw so that only the scrapbook paper shows. Repeat to make more beads.

To Make a bracelet:

Attach a ball-chain clasp to a piece of ball chain long enough to fit around your wrist. String on paper beads and coordinating beads until the chain is filled. Close the bracelet by locking the final ball into the ball-chain clasp.

Earrings

decorative paper
punch

scrapbook paper

clear self-adhesive
vinyl paper

pad-post or
regular-post earrings

craft glue
(optional)

small hole punch
(optional)

Punchy Posts

Use punched paper shapes to make a style statement.

Using a decorative paper punch, punch out two identical shapes from scrapbook paper. Cover both sides of the punched-out shapes with clear self-adhesive vinyl paper. Trim each one, leaving a thin border of the vinyl paper. Attach the shape to a pad-post earring with a small dab of craft glue, or punch a small hole through the center of the shape and slip a post earring through to hold the shape to your ear.

Puffy-Sticker Posts

Turn decorative stickers into a stylish accessory!

Attach one puffy sticker to a piece of scrap paper. Trim off the paper around the sticker. Use a small dab of craft glue to attach a pad-post earring to the back of the scrap paper. Let dry. Repeat the steps to make a second earring.

Supplies

2 matching or coordinating puffy stickers

scrap paper

scissors

craft glue

pad-post earrings

Falling Snowflakes

These winter-themed earrings are *brr*-illiant!

 Slip one head pin onto a snowflake confetti embellishment through the precut center hole. Top the pin with two beads. With help from an adult, slip the end of the head pin through the bottom loop of an earring hook. Bend the head-pin end around the loop, or ask an adult to pinch the end closed with pliers. Repeat to make a second earring.

Supplies

2 snowflake
confetti
embellishments

2 1-inch head pins

4 beads

earring hooks

pliers (optional)

NeckLaces

pencil

scrapbook paper

scissors

chipboard

glue stick

hole punch

cord

sticker

breakaway clasp

Pretty Pendant

It's easy to add your personality to this pendant!

Trace a circle-shaped chipboard piece onto patterned scrapbook paper. Cut out the paper circle. Rub a thin layer of glue on the back of the paper, and place it on the front of the chipboard so that the edges line up. Make a small hole at the top of the circle with a paper punch. String a cord through. Attach a decorative sticker to the front of the pendant. Attach a breakaway clasp to each end of the necklace cord to wear.

small photo

adhesive frame

jump ring

cord

breakaway clasp

Picture Perfect

Now you can keep a pet or friend always close to your heart!

Stick a small photo to the back of an adhesive frame and trim edges. Attach a jump ring through the charm top and string a cord through it, or string the cord through the hole provided. Connect a breakaway clasp to each end.

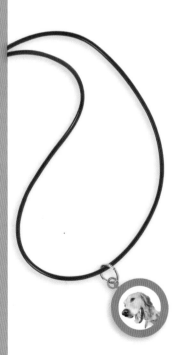

chipboard shapes

Glue Dots

embellishments
(optional)

2 jump rings

hole punch
(optional)

2 chains

breakaway clasp

Chipboard Cuties

Layer shapes to make a necklace that's as cute as can be!

Layer chipboard pieces with Glue Dots. The chipboard pieces can have preprinted designs, or you can decorate a plain chipboard piece with embellishments such as scrapbook paper, stickers, or adhesive gems. Attach jump rings to the prepunched holes in the chipboard pieces, or make holes using a hole punch. Attach one chain to each jump ring, and add a breakaway clasp to join the chains.

Tag It

Double the charms means double the style!

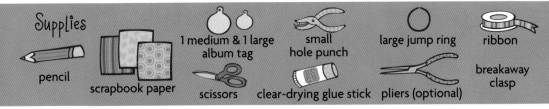

Supplies

pencil

scrapbook paper

1 medium & 1 large album tag

scissors

small hole punch

clear-drying glue stick

large jump ring

pliers (optional)

ribbon

breakaway clasp

1. Trace around one album tag onto scrapbook paper. Repeat with the other album tag on a separate sheet of paper. Mark the openings.

2. Cut out the shapes inside the traced line, and use a small hole punch to create the top holes in the paper.

3. Rub a thin layer of glue on the back of each album tag, and place it on the front of the matching paper shape so that the edges line up. Let dry.

4. Layer the album tags, and guide a large jump ring through the top openings.

5. Close by hand or ask an adult to close the ring with a pair of pliers.

6. String a ribbon through the jump ring, and add a breakaway clasp to the ends.

rectangular "best
friends" sticker

card stock

scissors

decorative-edge
scissors

hole punch

2 jump rings

necklace
(type is optional)

B.F.F. Necklaces

Make a pair of necklaces for you and your pal to wear.

Press a "best friends" sticker onto the back of a pretty piece of card
stock. Trim the card stock around the sticker. Cut down the middle
of the sticker with a pair of decorative-edge scissors. Punch one
small hole in the top middle of each piece. Attach a jump ring to
each charm top. Hang the charm on a necklace wire, ribbon, cord,
or chain.

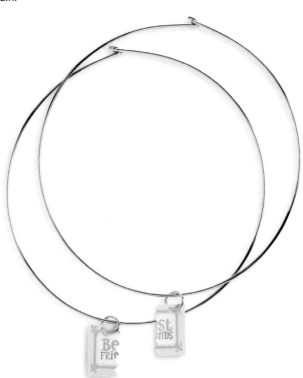

Rings and Things

rubber sticker

scrap paper

scissors

craft glue

plain finger ring

removable tape
(optional)

Rubbery Ring

This flexible sticker makes a really fun-looking ring!

Press a rubber sticker onto a piece of scrap paper. Trim off the paper around the sticker. Dab craft glue onto the back of the scrap paper and attach it to a plain ring. Let dry. (You may want to use removable tape to hold the rubber sticker in place while the glue dries.)

3 to 6 adhesive
gems

plain finger ring

Sparkly Ring

It's easy to add a little sparkle to your style!

Simply stick as many adhesive gems as you like or as will fit onto a plain ring. Use all the same color or mix colors to make different patterns. The options are limitless!

A Pin with Pizzazz

Pin on the perfect style!

Making a pin from a chipboard piece is as easy as sticking an adhesive pin back to the back of the chipboard. Add your personal touches by decorating with embellishments such as scrapbook paper, stickers, or adhesive gems.

chipboard letter
or shape

adhesive pin back

embellishments
(optional)

Chain-Link Belt

Create a chain of chipboard shapes to make a cute belt!

Punch a small hole on each side of each chipboard piece. Arrange the chipboard pieces as you'd like them to look as a belt. Link all of the pieces together using metal jewelry hooks, with 2 chipboard shapes linked by 1 metal jewelry hook. Link enough pieces to fit around your waist. Wear the belt over the top of a long shirt or around the middle of a dress.

Supplies

small hole punch

15 to 25 chipboard shapes (more or less, depending on waist size)

jewelry hooks (as many as needed for the number of chipboard shapes)

Straw Bead Bracelet Pattern

Use this pattern photocopied at 100%
for the craft on page 18.

Show us pictures of your Scrapbook Jewelry creations!

Send them to:

Scrapbook Jewelry Editor

American Girl
8400 Fairway Place
Middleton, WI 53562

(All comments and suggestions received by American Girl may be used without compensation or acknowledgment. Sorry—photos can't be returned.)

Here are some other American Girl books you might like:

❑ I read it.

❑ I read it.

❑ I read it.

❑ I read it.

❑ I read it.

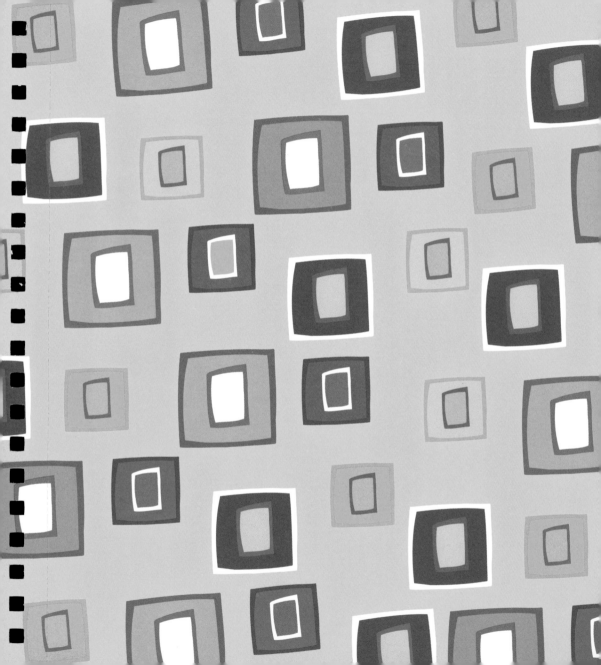

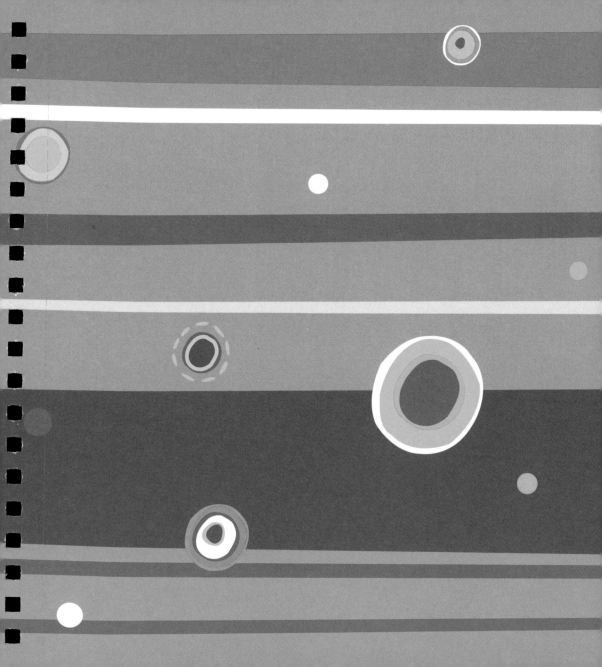

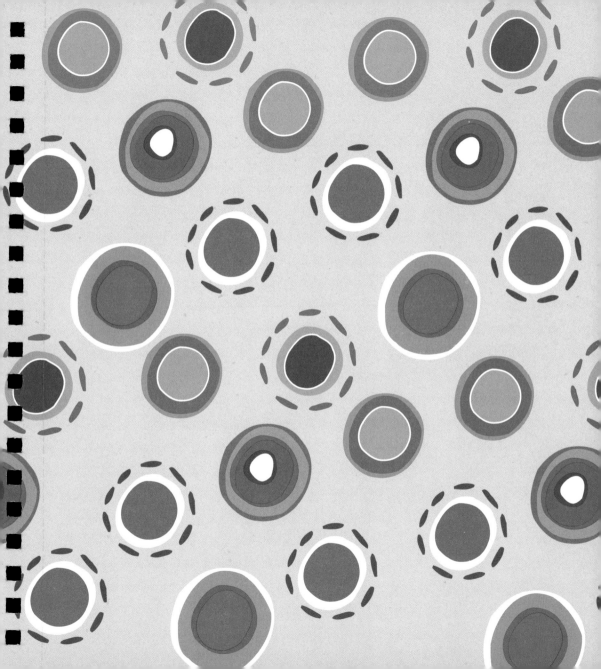